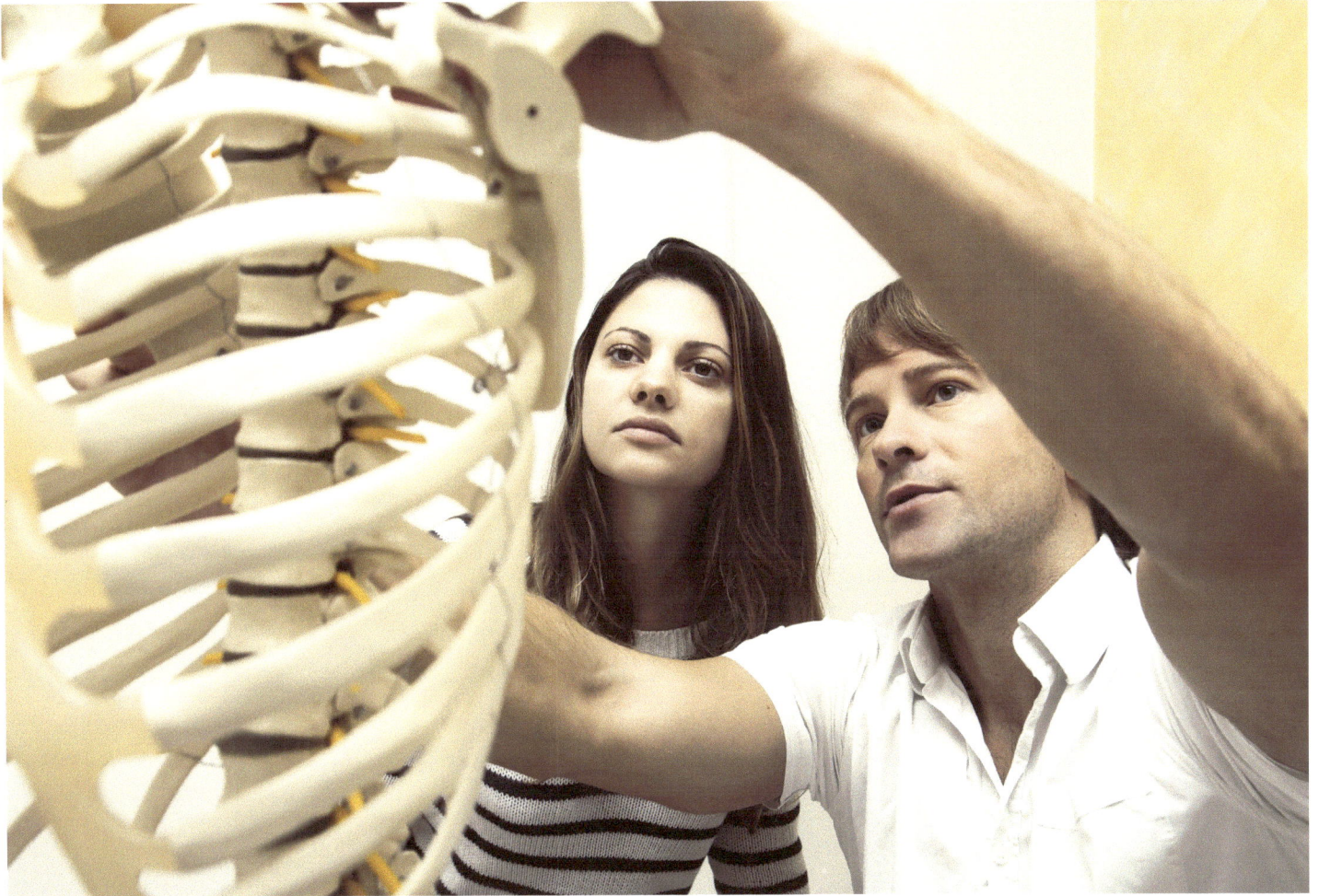

U.S. Copyright Office the Library of Congress

Please respect the information in this book is copyrighted — it is unethical and illegal to dispense any part of this material.

Violation of copyright laws and usage warnings can result in revocation of professional licenses, legal penalties and fines.

You must be certified and receive written permission to teach, copy, scan, digitally transfer or share this document or any of the information in part or whole. No part of this publication may be stored in a retrieval system, transmitted in any form, by any means, or reproduced or redistributed in any way, and no part may be copied or quoted in any publication, without the direct written permission of Dr. Michael Koplen.

Thank you for abiding by these copyright agreements.

ISBN# 978-0-9996270-4-4

Disclaimer

While no one can predict how successful your connections with doctors or other practitioners might prove to be, benefits they might provide, or referrals they may generate, one thing that's for sure is when you develop professional relations with the right doctors, it increases the likelihood of successful outcomes and enhancing your professional credibility.

Dedication

This Course is dedicated to Massage Therapists who desire to practice massage in a complementary manner with other health care professions and cultivate a mutual respect for the uniquely important roles that various practitioners play in helping clients and patients.

"Your practice should not be competitive with doctors, but rather complementary!"

— Michael Koplen, MT, DC

Acknowledgment

My deepest appreciation goes to the dedicated teachers who inspire and guide us along our educational journeys.

"There is a place of respect for all forms of therapy in America today, and we must work together so we can successfully combine our talents to contribute to the order and well-being of our clients."

— Erik Dalton: Freedom From Pain Institute

"I am friends with, and refer personally to some of the most amazing Physicians, Chiropractors, Physical Therapists, Osteopaths, Podiatrists, Athletic Trainers, etc., in the medical industry. In return they share with me the missing link that is found with challenging clients, in cases where I did not have a solution. In other words they teach me their strengths to make me a better educator. With that said, I encourage massage therapists to seek out, and work with those top manual therapists."

— James Waslaski, International Speaker and Teacher, Founder of The Center for Pain Management, Massage Therapy Hall of Fame

Table of Contents

Introduction..1

Three Fundamental Ways to Connect With and Develop Professional Relationships with Doctors and Other Health Practitioners in Your Area...............................3

Here's How Your Practice Benefits by Developing Professional Connections with the Right Health Care Providers..5

How to Know if a Doctor is Competent and Trustworthy...6

How it Benefits You to Develop Professional Connections with DC's...........................7

Here's Why DC's Can Be Helpful..8

Why It's Beneficial for You to Receive Care from One or More DC's in Your Area..........9

Important Message About Spinal Adjusting..10

How to Introduce Your Practice to a Doctor...11

Important Concept to Know When Connecting with Doctors.....................................13

Here's How to Set Up a Meeting with a Doctor to Introduce Your Practice to Them......14

Three Important Messages to be Sure to Communicate to DC's.................................15

Potential Problem in Contacting the Doctor...19

Sample Phone Call to a Doctor...22

What to do if a Doctor is Interested in Meeting with You..25

List of Materials to Send to Doctors to Introduce Your Practice.................................26

Four Important Things to Be Sure to Include in Your Networking Letter to Send to Doctors...27

Networking Letter to Send to Doctors...28

How to Use the Massage Therapy Prescription Form...30

Conclusion..35

Introduction

If you're like most Massage Therapists you would like to professionally interact with doctors but you aren't sure how to do it.

You may want to connect with them for a variety of reasons, such as establishing mutual referrals so clients and patients can benefit from complementary care, to seek advice about a client's condition or refer them for evaluation, or to work in a doctor's clinic.

You may feel unsure or even intimidated about how to make such connections happen.

This straightforward book is designed to give you permission, persuasion, and strategies for confidently connecting with doctors, especially doctors of chiropractic (DC's) because they are trained to evaluate musculoskeletal and neurological symptoms and conditions that you may be uncertain of which warrant further assessment. And DC's can assist in releasing severe spinal fixations causing sustained neurological compromises that you might encounter.

My suggestions presented to you in this book come from having careers in both massage and chiropractic. When practicing massage along with other MT's, while owner of the Denver Massage Center, we established wonderful professional relationships with DC's to whom we referred clients, and they, in turn, referred patients for massage. These referrals generated hugely successful practices for us. Such referrals can do the same for you too!

In my current chiropractic practice, I recommend massage and other forms of manual therapy to all patients, and maintain relationships with an Orthopedic and Neurology group, a general practitioner MD, a Naturopath, Psychologists and an Acupuncturist.

Several Massage Therapists we refer patients to have solid practices filled with clients. So I know from firsthand experience you too can benefit from having good professional connections with doctors!

Most beneficial connections with doctors are created by doing two things: knowing how to implement the right strategies to develop successful professional relations with them, and by persisting in your efforts to reach out to them. Your persistence in implementing the right strategies is what creates the right connections — otherwise, they are unlikely to just randomly happen.

This book shows you solid strategies for connecting with the *right* doctors, in the right way. But you are the only one who can implement them. You'll be glad you did because establishing such connections is sure to increase your professional credibility, respect, and overall practice success. The massage *profession's* credibility and notoriety will benefit too.

So step out of your comfort zone, go beyond your hesitations and fears, and feel confident in reaching out to doctors by applying the insights provided for you in this book!

NOTES: I exercised poetic license and left out the periods in various practitioners' titles for simplicity, such as MD or DC. Also, chiropractic and osteopathy are referred to synonymously in this book.

Feel free to creatively modify and edit the materials in this book to best accommodate and complement your particular practice style and needs.

"I know that effective thinking does not occur just because something is said. An insight must be repeated, and repeated, and repeated again. Only then, when it is fully accepted and understood, do you begin to alter behavior."

— Dr. Wayne Dyer

Three Fundamental Ways to Connect With and Develop Professional Relationships with Doctors and Other Health Practitioners in your Area

1. Call Them to Introduce Your Practice.
2. Mail Information About Your Practice to Them.
3. Refer Clients to Them.

This book shows you how to do the first two. (Another book, How to Professionally Refer Clients, teaches you how to refer clients for evaluation when needed in ways that encourage doctors to have them return to you for further care.)

The doctors you're most likely to interact with and who will be your strongest allies for offering you advice and sending you referrals are osteopaths and chiropractors because they work with musculoskeletal and neurological issues similar to ones you see with your clients.

This book places attention on connecting with DC's because they are less pharmaceutically inclined than osteopaths, and they tend to work in a more integrated manner with conditions that massage treats.

Experience has also shown that DC's are far more likely to refer patients to you.

But exercise great caution in referring a client to a DC for evaluation without first connecting with them or understanding their style of practice, if possible. You will soon be shown why this is important.

Learn how to co-manage clients and patients seen by DC's, at IntegrativeCareMastery.com

Your first step is to decide what type of doctors you want to connect with and create a database with their contact information.

There is a tendency to want to try to connect with "any and all" health care providers in your area, but it's best to selectively choose which ones you want to network with instead of reaching out to everyone.

Choosing who to connect with is a personal choice. You may feel more comfortable connecting with certain Chiropractors, Osteopaths, or types of MD's. You may also choose to connect only with practitioners who are in close proximity to your practice, because clients sometimes prefer the convenience if they can avoid long drives across town, especially in larger metropolitan areas.

You can search for and collect providers' names, contact information, and specialties by using Google or other search methods. In the past the phone book has proven helpful in annually deleting providers who are no longer listed. Providers relocate, so it's important to periodically update your database.

Use whatever system you prefer to manage your database, such as SalesForce, Filemaker, HighRise, Excel spreadsheet or whatever is easiest for you.

Here's How Your Practice Benefits by Developing Professional Connections with the Right Health Care Providers

There are several reasons why developing professional connections with the right health care practitioners can benefit your practice. One is they are readily available to help you at times when you need to seek advice from them.

It's beneficial for your massage practice to have good working connections with at least one DC and MD in your area because clients' conditions can warrant evaluation from these practitioners — and it's good to know who you can confidently refer a client to when necessary.

The type of MD's who you will most likely be referring clients to or seeking advice from are orthopedists, neurologists, neurosurgeons, general practitioners, and gynecologists. Obstetricians and gynecologists can be strong mutual referral sources, because clients sometimes present with concernable abdominal or back related pain, and massage is often recommended for pregnant women.

As you start connecting with doctors and others with whom you share mutual respect, your credibility and professional esteem will increase. So will your referrals and practice success!

Your clients will also appreciate you more when you refer them when appropriate. They will view you as having greater professional credibility, trust you more, and be more apt to refer others to you.

Learn how to co-manage clients and patients seen by DC's, at IntegrativeCareMastery.com

How to Know if a Doctor is Competent and Trustworthy

The truth is there is no way to know for sure if a doctor is trustworthy or competent. But there are signs that can help you discern if they are supportive of massage and have a good reputation with treating patients.

The best ways are by word of mouth from others who have experienced a particular doctor, especially colleagues or clients. If you're savvy using Yelp or other such sources you may be able to decipher real reviews from phony ones or paid ads.

The next few pages explain why it's beneficial for you to visit with and even receive treatment from a DC so you can judge their competency and practice style firsthand.

When you communicate with a doctor's staff or the doctor her/himself by phone, you should be able to tell quite readily if the doctor is a massage ally by using the scripted dialogues presented later in this book. That's a great first step because you do not want to waste your time with a doctor who is not supportive of massage, and instead move on to finding and connecting with other practitioners who are.

Too many Massage Therapists waste their time and energy trying to "convert" resistant practitioners to like or accept what they do. This is not a good approach because it requires too much effort – and the chances are slim you will end up changing their mindsets – plus it can leave you emotionally drained and bummed out.

If you happen to find yourself interacting with a health care practitioner (HCP) who is rude to you or the massage profession, strive to remain polite but don't waste your time continuing to converse with them. Instead, focus on interacting with and establishing relations with practitioners who support you and your practice.

Learn how to co-manage clients and patients seen by DC's, at IntegrativeCareMastery.com

How it Benefits You to Develop Professional Connections with DC's

Chiropractors can be good sources for you to establish mutual referral systems for several reasons.

1. Client conditions can sometimes present to you that are outside your scope of practice, which require advice that DC's can often help with.

2. Client conditions may warrant chiropractic evaluation.

3. DC's can be great sources for answering client management questions.

4. Some clients you see may also be receiving chiropractic care, so it's important for you to be knowledgeable about its integrative nature with massage.

By establishing trusted connections with one or more DC's, you can refer your clients to them when necessary and trust the DC will:

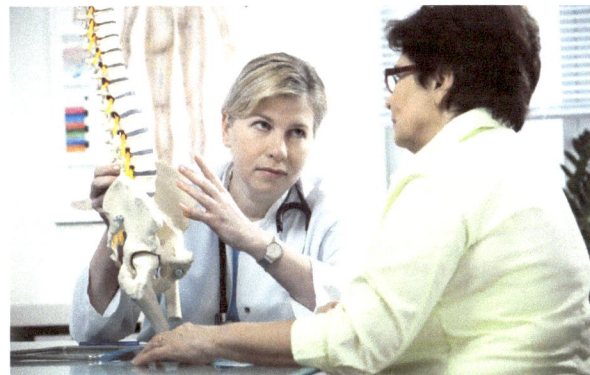

- Respect you and massage therapy.

- Provide your clients with quality evaluations.

- Provide your clients with quality treatment, if necessary.

- Support your clients in continuing to receive massage from you.

Chiropractic care complements massage and clients often benefit from both therapies integrated into their treatment.

NOTE: Chiropractic research studies for a variety of conditions can be found at chiro.org.

Here's Why DC's Can Be Helpful

DC's can often help evaluate difficult or concernable client issues that present to you which are outside your scope of practice because the educational requirements for doctors of chiropractic are among the most demanding of any of the health care professions.

Most students already acquire four years of pre-medical undergraduate college education, including courses in biology, inorganic and organic chemistry, physics, psychology and related lab work.

Chiropractic college education requires four to five academic years of professional study in courses such as anatomy, physiology, Xray, biochemistry, lab analysis, orthopedics, neurology, physical examination, physical therapy, nutrition, public health, diagnosis, and spinal and soft tissue evaluation and treatment techniques.

Chiropractic college curriculum provides a minimum of 4,200 hours of classroom, laboratory and clinical experience, which is approved by the U.S. Department of Education.

DC's education is more intensive than their MD counterparts in many musculoskeletal related courses, treatment techniques, and includes at least a year of clinical patient care.

DC's are allowed to practice in all fifty states and most nations, and must pass rigorous state and national board exams, and in many states are required to take at least 24 hours of continuing education courses annually.

Doctors of chiropractic are considered primary health care physicians along with medical doctors and osteopaths, are licensed to diagnose health care problems, treat conditions within their scope of practice, and refer patients when appropriate for further evaluation or to other health care providers.

Why It's Beneficial for You to Receive Care from One or More DC's in Your Area

Receiving chiropractic care helps you gain a greater understanding of chiropractic principles and how chiropractic works.

Receiving chiropractic care also lets you determine if you like a particular DC's professionalism, personality, clinic environment, competency and practice style. If you don't like these aspects about a particular DC, chances are your clients won't either.

Other things you may want to explore about a DC may include:

- Do they use physical therapy modalities?
- What type of self-care strategies do they recommend to patents?
- You will be able to feel out the DC's adjusting technique, which helps you determine if their technique is appropriate for a client you may need to refer. For example, some DC's use "low-force" techniques, while others adjust spines more vigorously. Some clients may ask for a particular adjusting style, or you may have reasons why you want a client to receive a certain type of chiropractic treatment. Typically, clients with more severe spinal fixations require stronger force adjustments.

NOTE: Although the term "spinal manipulative therapy" (SMT) represents a broader scope of treatment approaches than the terms manipulation and adjustments, they are all often used synonymously, and refer to manual or other applications that release spinal related joint fixations, including costovertebral and costotransverse joints. I prefer the term adjustment rather than manipulation because it implies a more precise amount and direction of force applied.

Important Message About Spinal Adjusting

The amount of force required to properly adjust and release fixated vertebrae varies.

In some cases low-force techniques are sufficient, while others require stronger directed force.

The degree of force necessary to release and restore proper mobility and function is proportional to the severity and degree of vertebral fixation, plus other factors such as related soft tissue restrictions.

Mild fixations can often be mobilized with very low force. You've probably experienced hearing a slight popping sound when mild joint fixation released while stretching or massaging a client. Simply twisting, bending or stretching often allows mild facet fixations to loosen or pop free.

In more serious cases of joint fixation, a stronger force is required to successfully release them.

"In some chronically locked vertebral segments...the Myoskeletal Method is not successful in restoring normal motion to the joint. If a few attempts do not succeed, a referral is made to a chiropractor or manipulative osteopath for a high velocity/low amplitude adjustment."

— Erik Dalton, Myoskeletal Alignment Techniques

How to Introduce Your Practice to a Doctor

Two ways to introduce your practice to a doctor:

1. Meet with the doctor and give them information about your practice and massage therapy.

2. Mail information to them about your practice and massage therapy.

It's important to know which materials to send.

While there are limitless choices of information to choose from to send to doctors, the specific ones that are provided in this book for you to use are recommended. Feel free to select from these choices, modify them as needed, and if necessary add other information to this list that you feel is relevant and important to your practice.

Try to provide doctors with specific pieces of information that you feel best support your objectives for meeting with them, and best represent *your* practice, instead of just giving them miscellaneous, general information about massage.

For example, you may want to give an MD research studies that show how massage helps reduce pain, anxiety, depression and tension.

You may want to show a DC how patients become more relaxed and less anxious when they receive massage, and how this and other benefits that massage provides can leave them more satisfied with their overall care with the doctor.

Use the information provided in this book along with additional information you feel may be helpful, such as appropriate educational pamphlets and articles.

It's a good idea to become familiar with the research literature and collect supportive studies and articles, so you can send appropriate copies to particular doctors and give copies to your clients. (This is discussed soon.)

NOTE: Massage Therapy research information can be found online through sites such as pubmed.org, massagetherapyfoundation.org, amta.org. and others.

After deciding which information to send, you need to know how to present the materials and the best time to do it.

If you are going to meet with a doctor, you can mail them some or all the materials before the meeting, or you can wait and give the materials to them when you meet with them. This will all be discussed soon.

Remember, it's the *quality* of information you deliver that matters most — not the quantity!

Important Concept to Know When Connecting with Doctors

The truth is, most doctors aren't as interested in hearing about your massage skills as they are knowing other considerations that are more important to them, which we'll list in a moment.

Here's the mistake most Massage Therapists make when trying to convince doctors how good they are: They try to impress them with how great their hands-on skills are, the number and names of all the techniques they know, and what terrific healers they are.

It's not that there's necessarily anything wrong with this. And of course, doctors want to know if you have a specialty and that you are competent.

But what they care about most is knowing that you can provide the type of treatments they recommend for patients they refer to you!

They want to know you are capable and willing to provide massage treatments that satisfy the care they recommend for patients. And they want to be assured that your treatments are integrated with the care they provide for these patients, or at least aligned with the care they prescribe for patients they refer to you.

So it's extremely important for you to let the doctor know they can trust that the work you will provide for patients they refer to you complements the type of treatments they provide or recommend for them!

Here's How to Set Up Meeting with a Doctor to Introduce Your Practice to Them

Let's assume you are connecting with a DC.

Two Ways to Set Up the Meeting

1. Call the DC by Phone.

The purpose of your phone call is to:

- Introduce yourself and your practice to the doctor.
- Request to meet with them.

2. Mail Them Information about Your Practice.

The purpose for mailing them information is the same purpose as calling them:

- Introduce yourself and your practice to them.
- Request to meet with them.

Calling to invite a DC to meet with you is much more effective than only mailing information requesting a meeting!

CAUTION — Whether you call to talk to a doctor or only mail them information, both methods must communicate three important messages. If you don't include these three messages, it greatly reduces the likelihood of the doctor responding as favorably to your invitation.

Three Important Messages to be Sure to Communicate to DC's

1. First, let the doctor know that you have a basic understanding of chiropractic principles and you are aware of the benefits that chiropractic care provides for patients.

Try to get into a discussion with them about this.

Let them know you're a supporter of chiropractic care — you believe in it and you understand it helps patients primarily by releasing articular fixations and related nerve irritation. Discuss this principle, which is the essence of chiropractic care, for as long as the doctor wants to talk about it. This is an extremely important opportunity to create a bond with the doctor by sharing a mutual reality with them.

Next, let them know you are aware that massage and chiropractic are complementary, and when they are both provided to patients, patients are more satisfied with their overall care. And you understand that your role as an MT focuses on soft tissue treatment that is aligned with their suggestions, so the two of you are sure to work collaboratively.

(If you are interested in having an in-depth understanding of how chiropractic works, exactly what DC's do, and the neuro-physiological mechanisms of how massage and chiropractic work in a complementary manner, visit MastersInMassage.com® and look for the Integrative Care Mastery course.)

Keep in mind that most DC's do not care for a lot of discussion about the results that massage provides, or how patients get better quicker because of massage. Unless the DC opens up a discussion about such therapeutic benefits that massage provides, my advice is to not talk too much about it. Nonetheless, situations can vary and exceptions occur, so use your best judgment about how much to talk about this.

The truth is, what DC's want most is for massage to complement the chiropractic care they provide, so be careful not to give the impression that your massage work is superior or has magical therapeutic benefits that will impress patients more than their chiropractic care!

Please don't misunderstand my point — I'm NOT saying that massage is not as effective or perhaps even more beneficial than chiropractic treatment in some cases — but what I am suggesting is that when you professionally connect with a DC, it's far more beneficial for you to focus on the integrative relationship between massage and chiropractic.

Remember, most DC's primary reason for using massage is to help create greater patient satisfaction, which encompasses many dynamics.

Although increased patient satisfaction can very well come about from patients healing faster, or getting better results by receiving massage, patients often appreciate massage for other reasons too.

Whatever the case, satisfied patients are more compliant with care and are more likely to refer others, which certainly keeps you and the doctor more satisfied!

2. Assure the DC that it's "safe" for them to refer patients to you.

You must communicate with DC's in ways that assure them you will support and reinforce their patients' need for chiropractic care, and not "steal them away"!

Assure the DC that you will *not* try to convince their patients who they refer to you for massage, that they should be receiving more massage instead of chiropractic. Even though massage in many ways may be just as important, and in some instances even more-so than chiropractic care, it's still important to let a patient who is under chiropractic care and was referred to you, know that the role of massage is to *complement* their chiropractic care and not overshadow or replace or it!

3. Assure the DC you will provide patients with the massage recommendations they request.

Like we mentioned, one of doctors' biggest concerns is that you will not provide their patients with the massage recommendations they request, and instead just "do your own thing."

So it's important that you let them know that they can trust you will provide each patient with treatments that focus on the specific areas of complaint they recommend care for, and with the intentions they request, such as to help reduce pain and spasm, or provide stress reduction and relaxation.

Of course, you can consult with doctors about their recommendations for particular patients' care, especially when you are confused or have questions about it, or have reasons to believe other aspects or areas deserve attention.

The doctors I work with consult with the Massage Therapists about patients we refer to them, or at least write out our recommendations on a Massage Therapy Rx form. And we welcome the Massage Therapists' feedback about their sessions with these patients.

You are encouraged to do the same, respecting that some doctors like having such communication, while others are not too interested and just refer patients to you trusting that everything is going well unless they hear otherwise.

So when a doctor asks you what techniques or approaches you use, instead of telling them a direct answer initially, or telling them what a great healer you are, it's usually best to mention the benefits your massage work can offer patients they will refer to you, such as:

1. Provides complementary care which supports the doctors' treatments in an integrative manner.
2. General stress reduction and relaxation that provides patients with comfort and satisfaction.
3. Decrease muscle spasm and tension.
4. Provide soft tissue relief for injury and focal pain.

Learn how to co-manage clients and patients seen by DC's, at IntegrativeCareMastery.com

Let them know that you understand the importance of spinal-neural-soft tissue relationships, and how your role is to provide the soft tissue (ST) care they recommend so it complements the treatments they provide!

When you do describe to the doctor the massage techniques or methods that you use, it's best to not go into too much detail about them unless they ask you to.

Also, doctors are rarely impressed hearing about specialty techniques. They may feel bored or even intimidated if they don't know about a special technique you use, and rarely do they want to be schooled with a dissertation describing it. But if they ask you, then of course feel free to explain.

Instead of hearing names like "Esalen, Feldenkrais or Alexander Technique," what they want to hear is what we have been saying all along — that you are willing and know how to apply whatever massage approach is necessary to fulfill their treatment recommendations — which usually involves, for example, Swedish or other styles for relaxation, or MFR and orthopedic style massage for treating focal areas and injury.

If the massage method you use happens to be esoteric or exclusive, such as strict shiatsu done on the floor, reflexology, or some form of energy work, be upfront and honest about this with the doctor. Respecting the benefits such techniques can provide, they are not what doctors or patients are expecting, so it's important to be clear with them about this. Some doctors may be okay with any technique you use as long as it fulfills their massage recommendations, while others may feel different.

Every doctor and clinic situation is somewhat unique, so always be honest with them and use your best judgment about what information you communicate to them.

Just be sure to cover the three important messages we just went over!

Potential Problem in Contacting the Doctor

It can be difficult to get the doctor's front staff who answer the phone to put you through to speak directly with the doctor.

They may only allow you to leave a voicemail on the doctor's phone, or they may ask you to leave your message with them to give to the doctor.

Here's what to do. First, introduce yourself to the staff member:

- ▶ *"Hi (their name___), my name is Susan Goodhands and I'm a certified massage practitioner who practices here in town (say the location)."*
- ▶ *"I'm in private practice and I would love to meet with the doctor in charge at your clinic to discuss how my professional massage practice can help them, especially when I need to refer my clients to the doctor for evaluation."*

Questions to ask them:

- ▶ *"Is there a particular time that's best to call her/him so I can speak to them about referring clients to her/him?"*
- ▶ *"Is there a time that s/he sets aside to return calls, write reports and deal with correspondences?"*
- ▶ *"Does s/he typically return phone calls and/or messages such as mine?"*

After this opening dialogue, ask them:

- ▶ *"Does your clinic have Massage Therapists who work there?"*
- ▶ *"Do you know if the doctor refers patients out to any particular Massage Therapist?"*

Learn how to co-manage clients and patients seen by DC's, at IntegrativeCareMastery.com

Options to tell them, depending on the outcome of the conversation. Assuming they are friendly toward massage:

If you are interested only in referring clients for evaluation when the need arises and not interested in working in the clinic, tell them:

▶ *"I'll mail information to the doctor so s/he will be familiar with me when I need to refer clients to them for evaluation."*

If you are interested in working in the clinic, let them know:

▶ *"I'll mail information to the doctor so they'll know that in addition to my private practice, I'm also available to work shifts in your clinic if you have the need."*

Either way, continue to tell them:

▶ *"I am extremely qualified and reliable, should the doctor ever have the need to refer patients for massage."*

▶ *"I'll mail the information about myself to the doctor and please let them know that we talked and s/he should be expecting the information."*

▶ *"Would it be better for me to just send the information to you, for you to give to the doctor?"*

IMPORTANT TIPS: It's more advantageous to go by the clinic, meet the staff and personally drop off the information.

You may want to offer the front staff person the opportunity to receive a massage from you — complementary (free) or at a discounted rate — if you feel this might encourage them to recommend you to the doctor.

This way, they can experience your skill level and professionalism, and you develop a relationship with them.

They may occasionally come across patients who are looking for a Massage Therapist outside of the clinic (especially if the clinic does not offer massage), and can become a referral source for you. They may even become a client of yours.

If you can get through to speak with the doctor, or when leaving them a voicemail, your phone call has two important goals:

- Introduce yourself and your practice.
- Request to meet with them.

KEY POINTS:

If you're speaking with the doctor and they start talking about other topics, give them plenty of time to discuss them. Conversationally engage with the doctor as much as you like — do not cut them off, or try to divert or argue with them — give them plenty of talk time.

Try to be professional while also being light and upbeat.

If the doctor has time to keep the dialogue going, allow it to happen. In fact, try to create a conversational flow with them. This helps create a "bonding time" with them. The longer you converse with them the deeper the connection that's being created between you.

Ask questions about their practice and chiropractic. You can talk about massage and your practice, but as we've mentioned, talking too much about your massage expertise or certifications can bore them or even intimidate them.

What they really want to know is that you are competent, reliable and professionally trustworthy — especially when it comes to providing their patients with the type of massage they prescribe and complements their chiropractic care!

Learn how to co-manage clients and patients seen by DC's, at IntegrativeCareMastery.com

Sample Phone Call to a Doctor

▶ *"Doctor _____, hi, my name is Susan Goodhands.*

  I'm a certified massage therapist who practices here in (say the location)."

▶ *"I'm in private practice and I would love to meet with you to discuss the nature of your practice and how my professional massage can benefit your practice (for example, by increasing your patients' overall satisfaction with their care with you; because everyone enjoys receiving a relaxing massage; I see you work with athletes and I provide sports massage, etc.)."*

▶ *"Also, I'd like to know if you're available when I need to refer clients for chiropractic evaluations. "*

▶ *"I'd love to meet with you briefly at a time that's convenient with your schedule."*

It's helpful to have some topics in mind before you call them to help create smoothly flowing conversation.

Here are some scripts that can open up topics to talk about:

▶ *"I'd love to hear about your style of practice."*

▶ *"I'd like to hear about spinal or other conditions you treat."*

▶ *"What type of care do you mostly provide?"*

▶ *"Do you take X-rays on your patients?"*

▶ *"I would like to have a doctor to refer my patients to for further diagnostic evaluations, and chiropractic treatments when necessary, and who also supports massage therapy. Are you interested in this?"*

▶ *"What role do you see massage plays in helping to reinforce or stabilize your chiropractic treatments?"*

Learn how to co-manage clients and patients seen by DC's, at IntegrativeCareMastery.com

▶ *"Do you currently utilize massage therapy to enhance your patients' satisfaction with their care? If so, how?"*

▶ *"Do you use massage therapy in your office?"*

▶ *"Do you refer patients for massage or recommend it to them? Where do you suggest they go?"*

IMPORTANT POINT: If you get through to the doctor, it's important to quickly find out if they are interested in massage and support it, or if they have a resistant or negative attitude toward it.

We have mentioned how it's important for you to recognize that if they aren't interested in massage or have a negative attitude toward it, accept this for what it is, do not waste your time trying to convert these doctors, and move on to finding ones who are interested in massage!

Here are some reasons why some doctors may support massage but not be interested in your offers:

- Some doctors already have Massage Therapists working in their clinic and do not need to refer their patients out for massage.
- Some doctors are afraid to refer their patients for massage because they are concerned about the quality and type of care the Massage Therapist will provide.
- Doctors fear that their patients may "switch over" to receiving massage and not return for their chiropractic care, or not follow through with their recommended program of care.
- Any of these reasons, as well as other reasons you may never know about, can keep doctors from wanting to meet with you or refer their patients to you.
- Sometimes the reality is that there is nothing that can be done to change their minds and persuade them otherwise. In such cases, it's best to simply thank them for their time, and reach out to other doctors!

If a doctor is friendly but NOT interested in meeting with you, or if you can only leave a voicemail, here's what to say:

▶ *"I'm going to send you information about my practice, so feel free to keep it on file in case you ever need a trustworthy and competent Massage Therapist to help you out, and so you will be familiar with me when I need to refer clients to you for evaluation."*

Next, you can mail the doctor some basic information about your practice in case they change their mind or ever have a need for a Massage Therapist.

Whatever appropriate materials you send, it can only be a positive and beneficial thing to do, and costs you nothing more than the paper and postage required.

At the least, you're getting your professional name out there and becoming better known, and have developed a relationship in case you need advice or need to refer a client for evaluation.

What to do if a Doctor is Interested in Meeting with You

Establish a date, time and place to meet with them.

- First, ask the doctor where they would like to meet.
- A great place is at their office because many doctors like to meet there and show you around. Others like to meet somewhere else, especially during their lunch break.

Call the doctor one or two days before your scheduled meeting date to make sure:

- They remembered their appointment with you.
- They are still available to meet with you.

Whether you call to meet with a doctor or only mail them information about your practice, in either case, you can select which materials to present to them from the same list of information.

List of Materials to Send to Doctors to Introduce Your Practice

- Your Networking Letter (provided for you in this book).
- Massage Therapy Prescription Form (provided for you in this book).
- Research Supporting Massage*.
- Your Professional Card.
- Your Resume (curriculum vitae).
- A copy of your Massage School Certification Training Diploma.
- If you have another relevant certification, such as the Integrative Care Mastery Course Certification from Masters In Massage.

TELL THEM:

▶ *"I'm certified in a special course, designed and taught by a Chiropractor and Massage Therapist, that trains Massage Therapists how to practice in a complementary manner with chiropractic. The course taught me an essential understanding of chiropractic principles, what your role as a DC is in helping patients, and what my complementary role is in providing them with massage."*

*There are many resources that can provide you with research studies that prove various benefits that massage provides, some of which were previously mentioned.

While you can select articles supporting the general benefits massage offers, it's more effective to send doctors specific articles that are aligned with and support the type of practice they have as well as a particular massage specialty you might practice. For example, if you specialize in sports massage, include articles that support its proven benefits. If you specialize in massaging pregnant clients, and especially when you are send information to an O.B.G.Y.N., provide them with articles that support the safety and benefits massage provides for these women.

Four Important Things to Be Sure to Include in Your Networking Letter to Send to Doctors

There are several important messages we have mentioned that should be included in your networking letter. If you fail to include these key messages, it's unlikely the doctor will respond as favorably.

It's a good idea to have someone proofread your letter before sending it, to check for grammatical errors, typos, etc. If it's not presented well, it can be a real deal breaker because it reflects poorly on your professionalism.

1. Introduce yourself.

2. Explain your understanding of what chiropractic care provides for patients and how massage therapy complements it.

3. Assure the DC that it's safe for them to refer patients to you. This is done by letting them know:

- You will support patients' chiropractic care that the doctor is providing for them.
- You will provide patients with the type of massage the doctor prescribes.
- You are not "competing" with the doctor or their treatments – you understand that your goal and role is complementary with the care the doctor provides.
- You will not be giving advice to patients the doctor is unaware of, or advice that may challenge or contradict what the doctor has suggested.

4. Give the DC incentives for interacting with you. *Let them know that by having their patients receive massage from you it will increase their satisfaction, which increases retention and referrals!*

Following is a custom designed networking letter you can send to doctors. Modify it as necessary to best represent your goals and practice style.

Networking Letter to Send to Doctors

Susan Goodhands, CMP
123 Network Avenue
Anywhere, CA 99999

March 4, 2020

Dr. Seymore Backs
123 Health Way
Somewhere, CA 95060

Dear Doctor Backs,

My name is Susan Goodhands and I'm a Certified Massage Practitioner.

I'm in private practice and invite you to see how my professional services can benefit your chiropractic practice with increased patient satisfaction, referrals and retention.

Although most Chiropractors are aware of the benefits professional quality massage provides, many of them don't have the time or desire to employ this adjunctive therapy in their office. Whether this is your situation, or if you are looking for additional massage in your clinic, here's what I can offer you:

I understand and respect how most chiropractic patients suffer from soft tissue tension resulting from spinal fixations and nerve irritation. While your primary focus is to correct these issues, my focus is to provide appropriate massage therapy to the areas that you, the doctor, determine are necessary – while reinforcing to patients their need for continued chiropractic care with you. *My role is to complement and support what you do.*

You can trust that my professional integrity will never leave you feeling anxious about losing your patients to another practitioner. You have my personal and professional commitment to supporting and reinforcing the need for your patients to follow through with their chiropractic programs of care that you recommend for them. I take this very seriously.

Most Chiropractors recognize that patients who also receive soft tissue massage actually become more dedicated to following through with their chiropractic care. They are also more likely to refer others to you because of their increased satisfaction with their overall care.

My practice is built upon quality, professional working relationships with clients, patients and health care providers. So if you have an immediate need or future interest in pre-scribing massage therapy for your patients, please contact me.

Likewise, I will presume that I may feel free to refer my clients to you whose conditions need further evaluation that is outside my scope of practice.

Sincerely yours,

Susan Goodhands

Susan Goodhands, LMT
456 Network Avenue
Anywhere, CA. 95060
(408) 458-1234

P. S. I have enclosed some information for you to review that further explains my professional qualifications and competency to work integratively with patients whose primary care is chiro-practic [including my certification to work in a chiropractic clinic].

How to Use the Massage Therapy Prescription Form

The Massage Therapy Prescription form is a very powerful tool.

It can be used in many creative ways to help increase your practice professionalism, credibility and referrals.

When introducing yourself and your practice to doctors, be sure to include this form in your packet of information. This form alone automatically encourages doctors to refer patients to you for massage and makes it much easier for them to do it. It's pretty self-explanatory.

You can make copies of this sample form and paste your contact information over mine. You can print your name and address at the top of the form, print the doctor's info, or just leave it blank.

TIP: Another way to use this form is to give it to a client who is going to a doctor for evaluation. Tell the client to ask the doctor to fill out their massage recommendations and have the client bring it to you when they return for their next massage session.

Michael Koplen, DC
4895 Capitola Rd, Capitola, CA 95010
(831) 475-6450

Massage Therapy Prescription

Doctor _____   Date _____

Patient _____   File# _____

M.T _____

AREA(s) of CHIEF COMPLAINT(s)_____

_____

_____

Dx _____

Focal Massage Areas

_____

_____

SOFT TISSUE
Tx RECOMMENDATIONS

Soft Tissue Intentions

❏ Inflammation

❏ Acute Spasm

❏ Contractures

❏ Adhesions

❏ ST Integration

❏ ST Stress Reduction

❏ ROM Therapy

Treatment Schedule

❏ 30 Minutes   ❏ 60 Minutes

❏ Daily ❏ Weekly   ❏ Monthly

Other _____

Number of Weeks _____

(Re-Evaluation)

Special Instructions: _____

_____

After sending your information packet, you can call the doctor a week to ten days later and say:

▶ *"Dr. Backs, I'm Susan Goodhands, the Massage Therapist who sent you my professional references last week."*

▶ *"I'm calling to make sure you received the information I sent to you."*

After they respond, make suggestions, such as:

▶ *"I would love to —*
Meet you...
Visit your office...
Discuss your practice...
Discuss how massage can increase your patients' satisfaction with your care...
Discuss referring clients to you for evaluation whenever necessary..."

If the doctor agrees to meet with you, set a date, time and place to meet with them.

It's a good idea to call the doctor one or two days before your scheduled meeting date with them to make sure:

- They remembered their appointment with you.
- They are still available to meet with you.

If a doctor does NOT want to meet with you, you may tell them:

▶ *"Thank you...I'm happy we had the chance to talk and connect... So please remember, if your patients – or anyone else you know – ever needs professional massage therapy, please feel free to call on me!"*

Here's a bonus strategy that can help a doctor increase their patients' satisfaction, while also getting them to send patients to you for massage.

Remember, doctors want to know why it's beneficial for them to interact with you and the massage therapy that you're offering. They want to know what's in it for them. It's your responsibility to convince them that interacting with you will ultimately increase their patients' satisfaction — not just with their massage care but with the overall complementary care they receive.

Offer the doctor a discounted gift certificate(s) from you that they can give as a free gift to one or more of their prized patients, or to a staff member.

For example, you can sell the doctor a one hour massage certificate for only $25, and they can give it to a patient as a free gift to show their appreciation to the patient for their loyalty. You can suggest they give one to a patient who is pregnant, who just had a baby, has referred many people, et cetera.

Some Massage Therapists prefer offering a doctor a *free* massage certificate. Free is a classic incentive, yet my opinion is it cheapens the appeal and makes you look somewhat desperate. I prefer offering discounted certificates in this situation. Do whatever feels best to you.

You can suggest to the doctor that they tell their patient:

▶ *"To show you my appreciation to you (for your ongoing commitment to chiropractic care), I want to give you this complementary gift certificate for a stress-reducing, relaxing massage."*

Tell the doctor this will bring exponential returns in patient gratitude and satisfaction — which is often reciprocated by increased patient retention and likelihood they will refer others.

You can suggest this idea to the doctor by writing it out as stated in the paragraph above and including it in your packet of information, or send it separately after having introduced yourself to them.

Even if they do not want to offer a massage certificate to their patients, they may give the gift certificate to someone else they know, such as a staff or family member.

However they choose to use it, it can ultimately bring a new client to you, or at least create a professional connection with the doctor where psychologically speaking, they may feel the desire to reciprocate with you in some way.

NOTE: Be careful about offering actual "gift certificates." A federal law was enacted in 2010 requiring the expiration on gift certificates to be five years. As of this writing, this law is still effective. Furthermore, the state law where you practice may be more restrictive, and if so, you are required to abide by the state law. Gift certificate laws usually reside on the side of the client – they are owed a service they paid for.

Learn how to co-manage clients and patients seen by DC's, at IntegrativeCareMastery.com

Conclusion

Please let this book serve as a valuable source of inspiration and strategies to connect with doctors.

Reaching out to connect with doctors will ultimately produce greater acceptance, credibility and referrals. It also helps to ensure that clients and patients receive optimum care.

If you would like to learn how to masterfully integrate your massage practice with chiropractic and osteopathic principles and practitioners, and practice along side these professions, visit IntegrativeCareMastery.com.

If you would also like to learn highly effective ways to get more quality referrals and increase your client retention without needing to advertise, visit RRMastery.com.

I wish you the very best of success and joy in your massage practice!

—Michael Koplen, MT, DC

Learn how to co-manage clients and patients seen by DC's, at IntegrativeCareMastery.com

About Michael Koplen

Michael Koplen, DC, MT, QME, is a teacher, practice management developer, Massage Therapist, National Chiropractor of the Year recipient through the prestigious Landis-Ward Practice Management group, and devoted husband and Father.

During his teenage years, Michael suffered from back and neck pain from a sports injury, but the medical doctors in his family only knew to offer pain meds. They were unaware of chiropractic or massage treatments to refer him to, which he eventually discovered and provided relief.

These and further experiences opened his awareness of the need for the various health care professions to connect with one another.

He experienced a life-changing trauma after college, and with his belongings in a small backpack, went to Boulder, Colorado, a mecca for New Age healing. He couch surfed in a household filled with Massage Therapists, Rolfers, Gestalt therapist, and yoga instructor while becoming immersed in exploring everything imaginable in the holistic health realm.

He completed the Boulder School of Massage Therapy's 1,000-hour program and was mentored in various Rolfing and MFR techniques. Committed to the mission of bringing a new era of massage professionalism to America, he opened the innovative Denver Massage Center were he practiced along with seven colleagues who "ate, breathed and slept" various forms of massage, while teaching massage classes at the massage center and through the Denver Education system.

Michael reminisces, "We established great professional relationships with DC's to whom we referred clients when the need arose. The DC's trusted referring patients to us for massage because we understood the integrative relationship between chiropractic and massage. We developed hugely successful practices through our mutual respect and referrals with the DC's, along with advanced client management skills we were learning."

Michael's clinical and personal experiences with massage and chiropractic, their relationships to the spine and nervous system, along with his is Father's untimely death from a spinal neuromuscular disorder, all inspired him to attend chiropractic college, where he furthered his assessment, treatment, and client management skills

In his chiropractic practice, he recommends massage to all patients and refers them either to Massage Therapists who work in the clinic alongside him and the other doctors or to ones in private practice who use specialty techniques.

Knowing first hand how beneficial it is for Massage Therapists to connect with doctors, especially DC's, he wrote this book to show you effective strategies. Because it's important for Massage Therapists to know how to professionally refer clients to doctors when the need arises, he wrote the companion book, How to Professionally Refer Clients.

He founded the Masters In Massage Institute®, has written several books for the massage profession, numerous articles, and developed courses for Massage Therapists that are available through home study and live classes that can be found at MastersInMassage.com.

Michael lives in Santa Cruz, California where he practices along with two other doctors, Massage Therapists, and an acupuncturist. His wife Alyson has a Psychology degree from UC Santa Cruz and practices massage in Medical and Chiropractic clinics. Their son Zak has a graduate degree from UC Santa Barbara's autism research center. Their daughter Alexis has graduate degrees from San Francisco and San Jose State University and works as a communications advisor at Oracle.

www.ingramcontent.com/pod-product-compliance
Lightning Source LLC
LaVergne TN
LVHW072112070426

835509LV00003B/121